W9-BOB-044

Almost
an
Animal
Alphabet

For Nas

Almost an Animal Alphabet
Text and Illustrations © Katie Viggers 2010
First published in Great Britain by Eightbear Press

All rights reserved. No part of this book may be reproduced in any manner in any media, or transmitted by any means whatsoever, electronic or mechanical (including photocopy, film or video recording, Internet posting, or any other information storage and retrieval system), without the prior written permission of the publisher.

Published by POW!
a division of powerHouse Packaging & Supply, Inc.

Library of Congress Control Number: 2013934868

37 Main Street, Brooklyn, NY 11201-1021
info@bookPOW.com
www.bookPOW.com
www.powerHousebooks.com
www.powerHousepackaging.com

ISBN: 978-1-57687-643-5

Book design by Katie Viggers

10 9 8 7 6 5 4 3 2

Printed in Malaysia

Almost an Animal Alphabet

By Katie Viggers

A is for Anteater
aarrgh
and ants

B is for bears

polar

black
(Asian)

sun

spectacled

bamboo
brown
black
(North American)
sloth
panda

C is for

Cat

d is for

Tyrannosaurus rex

Triceratops

dinosaur

Stegosaurus

Pterodactyl

E is for Elephant *(Indian)*

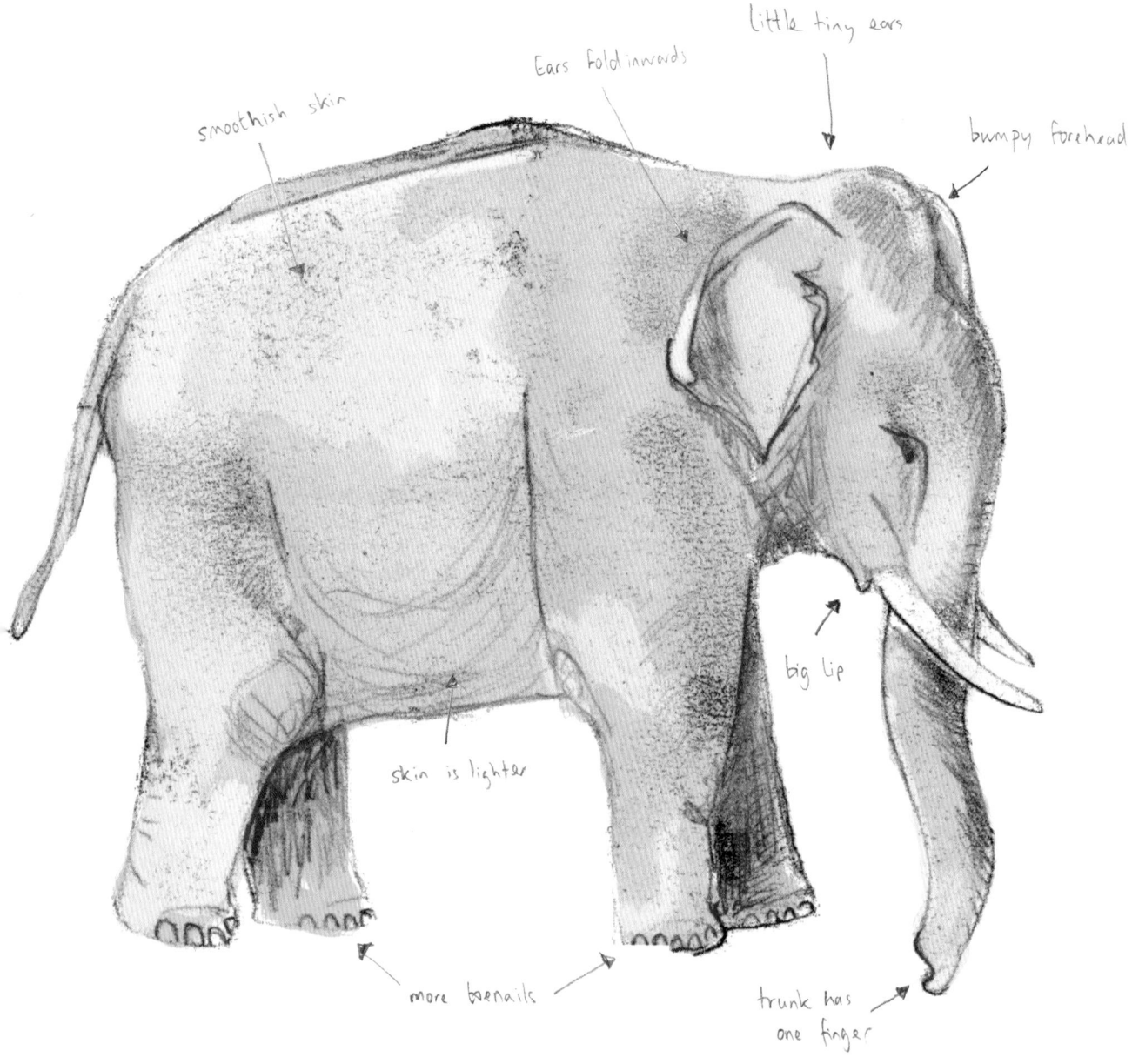

Elephant *(African)*

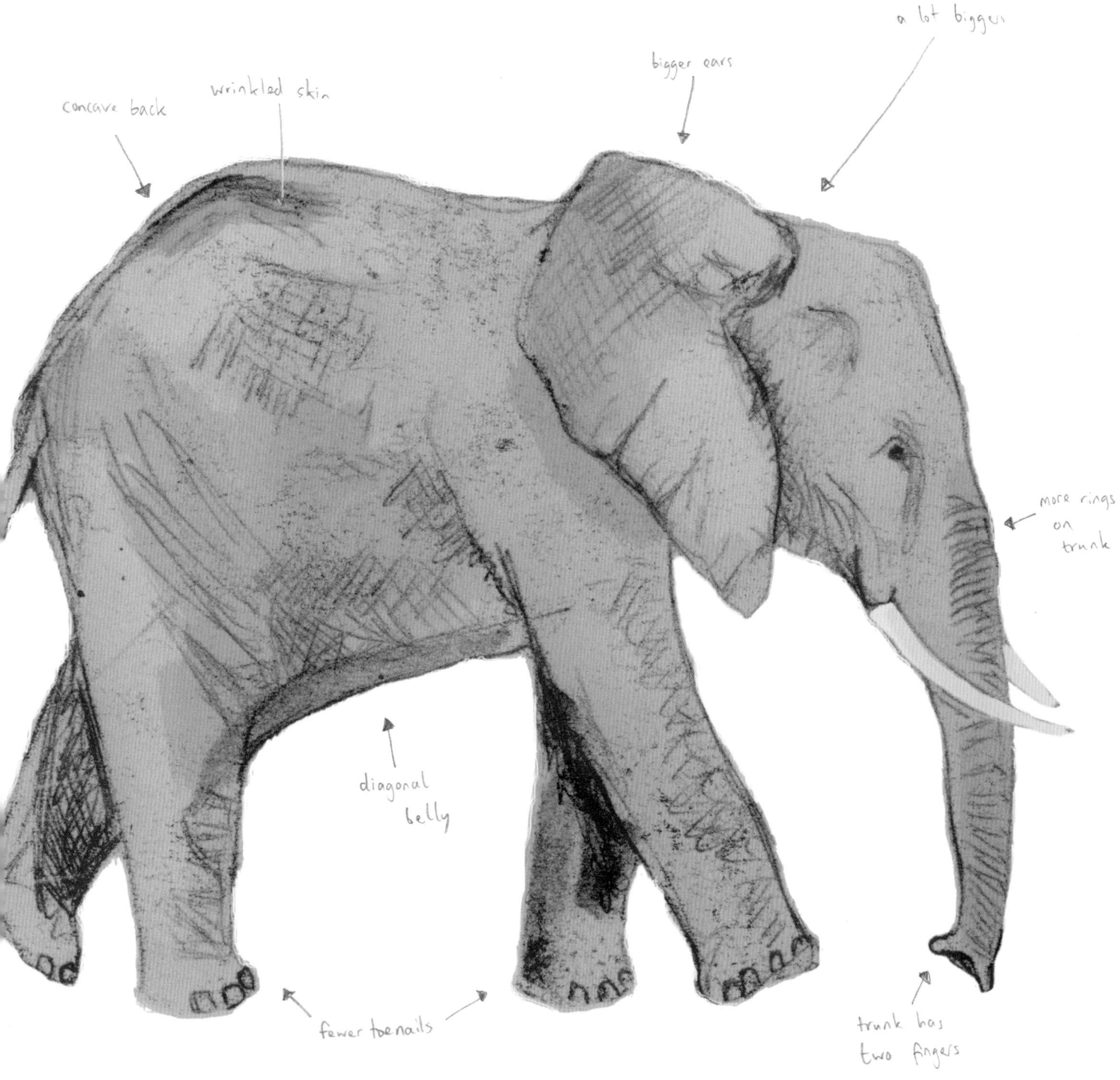

f is for fox
Arctic
fennec

Tibetan
red

G is for Gorilla

H is for
Hammerhead
Shark

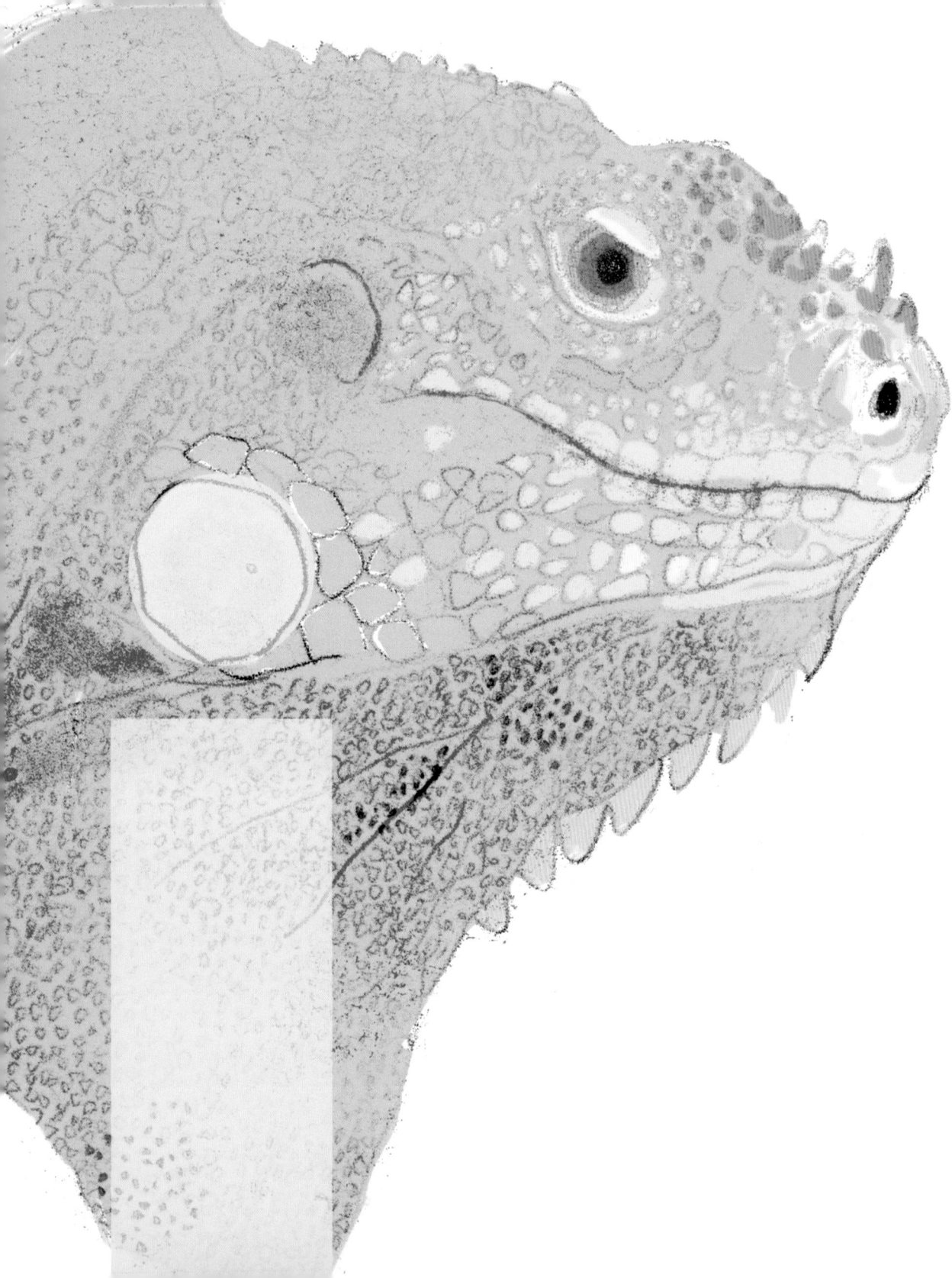

is for iguana

J
I S F O R

Jelly fish

K is for Koala

L is for Llama

colobus
capuchin
owl
spider
M

is for Monkey

n is for nighttime

O is for

Owl

P is for Penguins

Galapagos

little

Adélie king Fjordland rockhopper emperor

Q is for Quail

female

s is for sloth

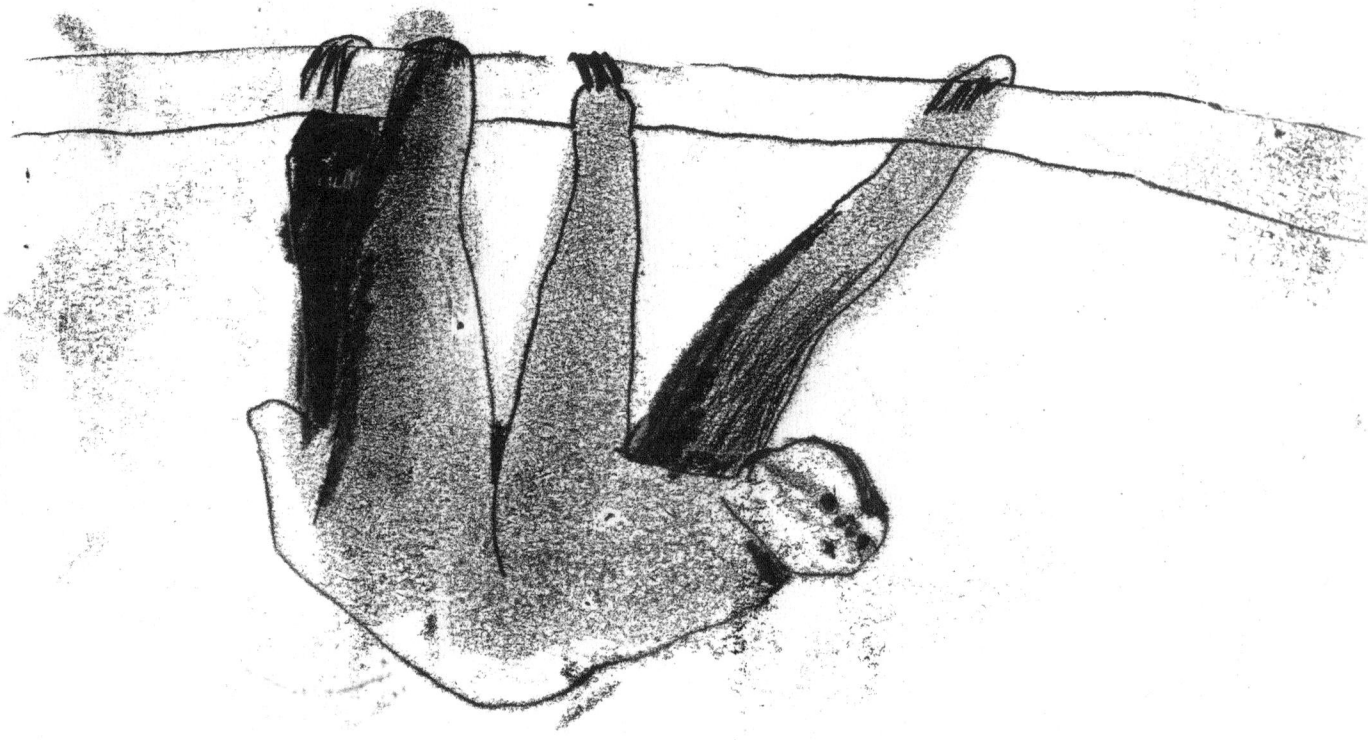

and snail

and seriously slow

t is for tarsier

U

is for **Underground**

v is for
Pondicherry
hooded

vulture
king
Rüppell's

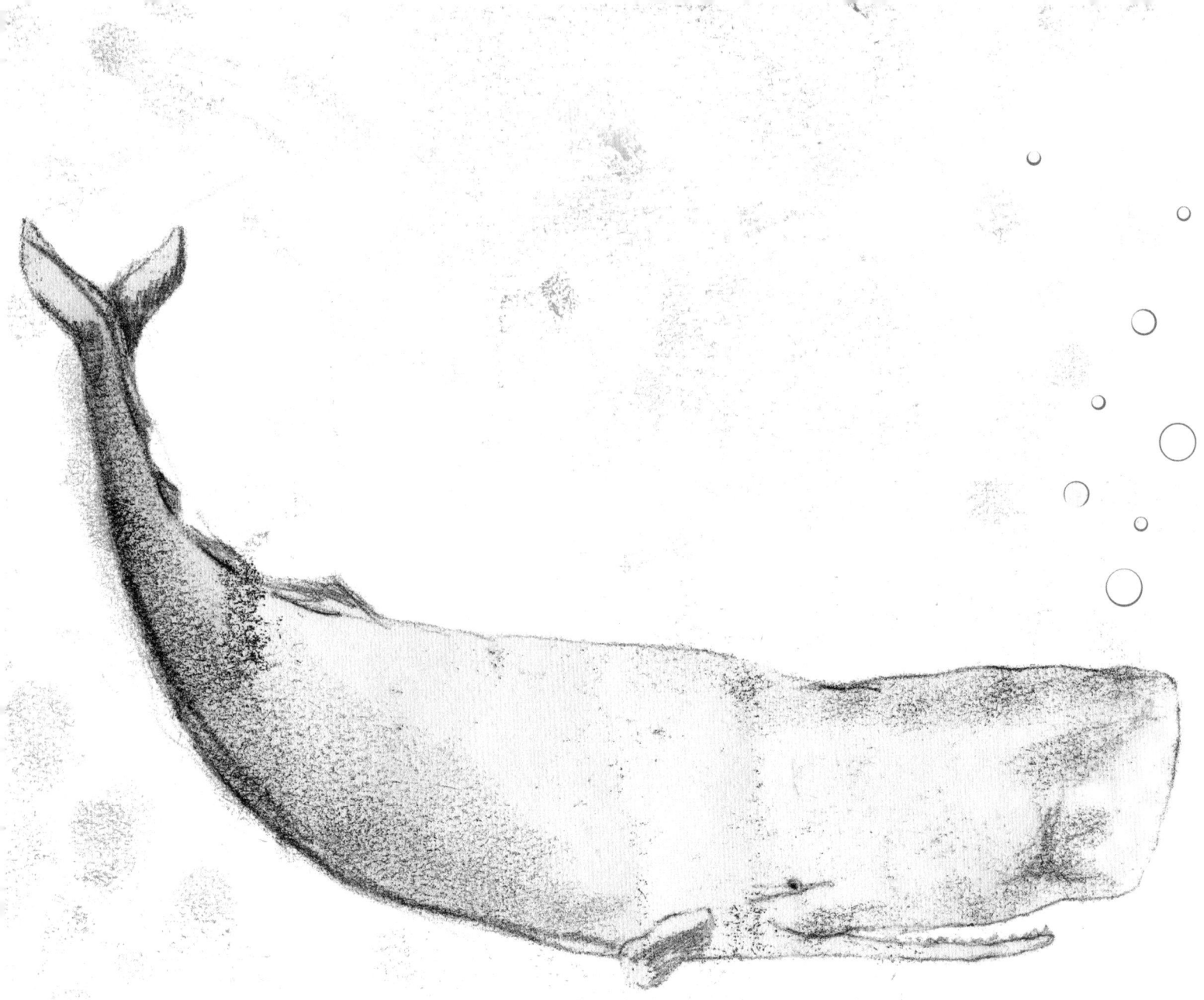

W

is for

whale

x is for x-ray

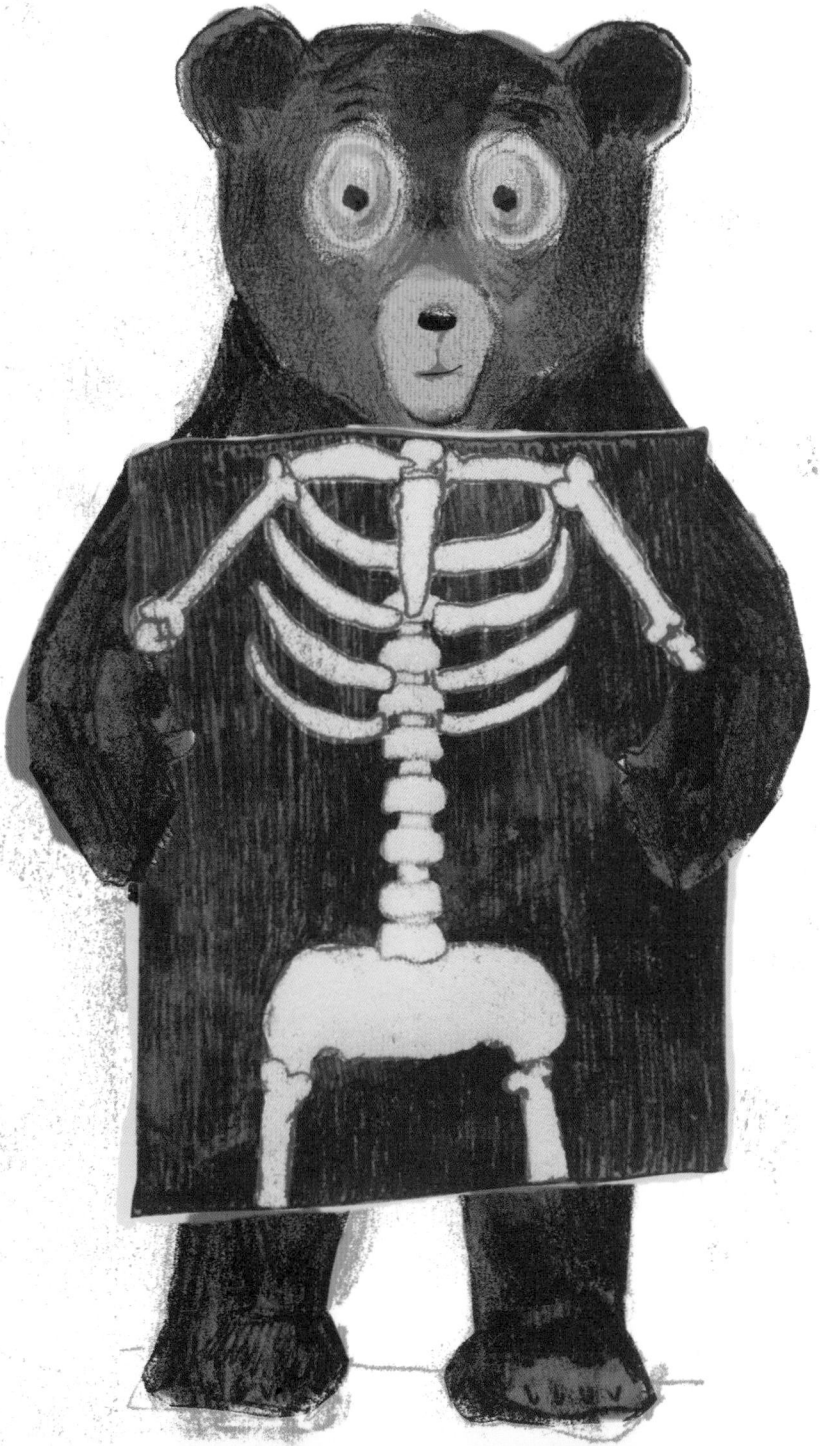

rah

Y is for Yeti

white
paint

Z is for zebra

KV is for Katie Viggers

Katie wrote this book 

She is an artist who lives in London, England

with her husband Nas and their cat Wally Molly 

… and the red foxes!